ANYONE'S GUIDE TO FINANCIAL SUCCESS

Nicholas Sovia

N Sovia Financial LLC

REVIEW REQUEST

Please consider writing a review for this guide on Amazon to help the creator and potential future readers. The average rating will directly affect how many lives it will impact. I hope you find it deeply informative and useful. Thank you.

Arguably the best form of financial security is trusting your ability to rise out of a poor financial status through your skills, intellect, and character.

CONTENTS

INTRODUCTION

This guide contains years of research and experience consolidated into a short, yet considerable explanation of today's best approaches to achieve financial security and success as well as approaches that have worked throughout history. It includes a unique, balanced combination of conceptual and factual information and statistics to draw conclusions of what are likely to be ideal paths for achieving various financial goals from various starting points. Adaptability of information is prioritized to accommodate people in virtually all financial situations and career paths. It provides exploration of the top investment vehicles that wealthy individuals have utilized to manage and build wealth in addition to other popular investment options and newer vehicles that may have significant potential going forward. Lastly, specific approaches to allocation of finances are discussed with multiple portfolio scenarios that are provided. Some points will specifically apply to those living in the U.S., but the concepts still hold true in other regions and most information will apply to global readers as well. There are some calculations and strategies that are relatively advanced, but if the reader takes the time to carefully review them, they will understand them. This guide is intended to be concise and straight to the point. Further research beyond this guide is encouraged for its readers in order for them to practice overall financial intelligence and discernment through the diversification of their sources of information. Independently reviewing charts online for various financial investments, especially in tandem with a compound interest calculator for estimating average annual returns, is a great way to avoid misinformation from other sources and confirm data presented in this guide.

FIVE MAIN CHARACTER TRAITS FOR WEALTH

1. Work smart
2. High risk tolerance
3. Patience
4. Resilience
5. Work hard

It requires working smart to choose good careers and investments. It requires a high risk tolerance to handle inevitable risk of failure and investment downturns. It requires patience for the approaches to play out. It requires resilience to navigate adversity. And it usually requires hard work to bring success to life.

Strength in some of these areas can sometimes make up for weakness in others. For example, the smarter you work, the less hard work you may have to do and vice versa, though working smart is more important than working hard, generally. The higher your risk tolerance is, the less patient you may have to be, because you can invest in more volatile investments that can yield faster returns.

TOP FOUR PRACTICAL PIECES OF ADVICE TO ANYONE

1. Pursue 1-2 realistic, high-paying careers you have passion for. Explore, research, and reflect until you find it or them. Consider your values. For many people, it is not so much about finding what you are obsessively passionate about in life, but finding what you are MOST passionate about or would be most content with. Before pursuing a career, ask yourself what the alternatives would be if you didn't pursue that career. If you can't think of anything that would be better for you, then it may be worth pursuing even if you may not be extremely passionate about it. You never know if you will become more enthusiastic about it while pursuing it.

2. Spend less than you make. Stick to a budget and avoid credit card debt that is not paid monthly as it is usually borrowing money to spend it rather than borrowing money to invest it, and interest rates on credit card debt tend to be very high.

3. When you can, invest savings primarily in your career(s) and secondarily in the Nasdaq 100 index and perhaps some optional real estate.

4. Avoid having children until you are already significantly financially successful, because their financial cost and time require-

ments to raise them will make achieving financial success much more difficult.

Please Note:
In order to get bank loans for businesses and real estate, you will want a good credit score, so using credit cards and always making payments on time will be important for building your score until you decide to get an actual loan. There are many different credit cards and it is important to research which ones are best for you based on your spending habits. If you can trust yourself to avoid credit card interest, then avoid credit cards whose strengths are lower interest rates and instead go for cards with better rewards or cash back on money spent.

PATHS TO ACHIEVE WEALTH

1. Work and invest

2. Entrepreneurship/business ownership (generally most profitable if you can do it)

3. Luck and privilege (Out of your control)

INVESTMENT VEHICLES AND MONEY STORAGE

INTRODUCTION TO INVESTMENT VEHICLES AND MONEY STORAGE

All investment vehicles other than certificates of deposit should be invested in with the preparation to hold them for the long term of at least 5-10 years, and therefore, they may all be perceived as highly illiquid (difficult to convert to cash) in that regard even though some are technically very liquid. Also, based on historical performance, they can experience drops of 30-100% and take years to recover, so patience and a high risk tolerance are nonnegotiable in investing. Investing in anything should be avoided until a few months or more worth of expenses is saved in cash for emergencies etc.

BEST INVESTMENT VEHICLES AND MONEY STORAGES AND REALISTIC EXPECTED ANNUAL RETURNS

1. Significant ownership of 1 or more businesses, 30%+
2. Real estate, 6-12%
3. Stock market, 12%+
4. Certificates of deposit and annuities, 2-5%

BUSINESS

Notes

Pros:

    Highest return potential (realistic 30%+ annually)

    Consistent income (not for angel investments or venture capital)

Cons:

    Highest risk.

    Highest level of involvement/responsibility

    Generally only suitable for people who have developed entrepreneurial talent

Individual Businesses

It is normal for a business to sell for 2 to 3 times its net earnings (earnings after expenses) ("Finding a Business"). Therefore, from earnings alone, and without borrowing money, **a 30-50% average annual return is realistic from owning a business, not including potential for business growth.** However, the degree of personal involvement, responsibility, and required expertise in the business will vary significantly and can be substantial. You can get a business loan from a bank and create very significant income with little initial capital. For example, if one could save up $50,000 for a down payment, it is possible for them to get a small business loan for $200,000 and buy an existing business that could make them an income of $100,000. It could be very dangerous to do this if you do not have expertise in the field of the business. If you want to start a business from the ground up, however, you will most likely need to use your own money or find an angel investor to get it started. Business ownership can be the quickest realistic way to become very wealthy. However, historical data suggests about 50% of U.S businesses fail within 5 years, and 65% fail within 10 years so there is definitely substantial risk (Gustafson, 2022).

Angel Investing/Venture Capitalism

If you are already wealthy, you can invest in businesses through angel investing and venture capitalism. Angel investing is direct investment in a startup company in its early stages, usually in exchange for partial ownership of the business (Goodshore, 2022). Venture capital funds on the other hand, are funds that pool money from multiple accredited investors (individuals who earn more than $200k a year or have a net worth over $1 million) and invest it into multiple private businesses in exchange for partial ownership for investors ('How to Invest," 2017). There is high potential for reward, but also very high risk and you may have varying degrees of responsibility in the businesses you invest in because you have partial ownership. These investments can go several years before yielding any returns and are highly illiquid. **Venture capital funds can yield average annual returns ranging from low single digit percentages to the mid 20s** ("Dividing the Pie," 2022).

Strategy

Only pursue if you have the interest to maintain and build whatever business(es) you start or buy.

REAL ESTATE

Notes

Pros:

    Realistic **8%+ annual return**

    Mostly passive to passive

    Consistent income/usually consistent growth

    Low risk

Cons:

    Very low chance of extremely significant returns in most cases

    Taxes on dividends and rental income

Average Annual Appreciation of U.S Homes (PK, 2022):

    1953-2022: 4.5%

    1972-2022: 5.3%

    1997-2022: 5%

Home prices have historically grown very consistently as a general trend, but the housing market crash that started in June 2007 and didn't fully recover until April 2016 is an example showing that it is possible for real estate to go long periods of time without consistent growth from home appreciation (PK, 2022).

Physical Real Estate

This guide will focus specifically on residential real estate investing for this section because commercial real estate investing (other than REITs, discussed later) will not be relevant to the vast majority of readers. It has been reasonable to rent out a property for 8-12% of what it is worth every year (Nicely, 2021). Depending on where it is located, it could be less. However, more recently, housing in many regions has appreciated much more than the cost of rent, making this number become more and more of a stretch in those regions. U.S homes historically appreciate about 4.5% a year (PK, 2022). After 1% home value annual maintenance costs, **a realistic long-term average annual return with a physical property is about 10-15.5%** (Nicely, 2021). The returns range should be a bit better if leverage (loans) is utilized with a 20% down payment, although there won't be much consistent income because most of the rent income will go toward the mortgage (loan) payments and maintenance. For example, if you buy a $300k home with a $60,000 down payment (20%) and it appreciates 4.5% annually, after 5 years the home will be worth about $374k. Hopefully you will have rented it out enough to cover the monthly costs. If you paid about $15,000 (5%) in closing costs and misc expenses when you first bought it, then you turned your $75k original investment into $134k of home equity (home value you possess after debt) in five years, which is a 12.3% average annual return. You may realistically make more than that by renting it out for more than your mortgage payment and keeping it occupied, potentially increasing **the average annual return rate to the upper teens through getting a home loan with a 20% down payment.** Use a mortgage payment calculator to estimate your monthly payments and avoid spending more than 35% of your gross income (before taxes) on loan payments (this debt-to-income ratio applies to business and personal loans as well). There are also FHA (Federal Housing Administration) loans you can get if you are eligible, such as the first time home buyer loan programs that can enable you to put as little as a 3.5% down payment for a home, which can yield extremely significant returns from home appreciation with a small investment ("First-Time Home Buyer Programs," 2022). The previous example of buying a $300k home with a 3.5% down payment could have turned a roughly $25k investment into $77k in home equity in five years, which is about a **25% average annual return with a first time home buyer loan.** However, as the home appreciates and the ratio of your home equity to the loan amount increases, your average annual rate of return on the investment will decrease due to less leverage. You can use a refinance to restart the loan and take out the cash you had paid toward the previous loan in order to keep utilizing maximum leverage and use your cash for other investments, however, you will not likely be able to cash out your home equity below 15% of the total home value via a refinance so the high return rate of the first time home buyer loan will only last a few years (Mortgage Info, 2022). After that you will proceed to make a much smaller, typical average annual return on your investment like in the first example.

REITs

Real estate investment trusts are funds that pool money from investors and invest in real estate (Chen, 2022). They are a great way to invest in real estate, especially commercial real estate, without extremely significant capital. Avoid publicly listed REITs that trade like stocks because their returns will likely depend far more on stock market fluctuations than fundamental real estate value and rental income itself (Vandenboss, 2021). Non-publicly listed REITs will vary in returns as well, but their **yearly dividends may range from 5-8% and capital appreciation may range from 2-5% (Morris, 2023) . A realistic long-term average annual return from non-publicly listed REITs could be 6-10%** (Morris, 2023). This might be a solid investment type for retirement passive income, not for growing your net worth.

Physical Real Estate and
REIT Comparison

Physical Real Estate:

Pros:

    Potentially higher returns than REITs

    More control over investments

    Tax write off potential from rental incomefor expenses (Boone, 2017)

Cons:

    Much more work/responsibility

    Much bigger initial capital investments required

Non-Publicly Listed REITs:

Pros:

    Passive

    Lower capital required

Cons:

    Potentially lower returns than physical property

    Less control over investments

    No tax write off potential from dividends like is possible with rental income

Strategy

Either invest in your own physical property or in non-publicly listed REITs, depending on your desired level of responsibility and involvement. It is important to do your own research on real estate in your specific region and its historical appreciation rates if you choose this route. Also, try to estimate the median rent price (where half are more expensive and half are less expensive) for homes in your area by looking at the current listings available. Then divide the median rent price in your area by the median home price to get a broad idea of what percentage of the home value you could charge for rent to tenants. It is also important to research which REIT may be best for you (search best non-traded REITs) depending on when you invest and whether you are an accredited investor or not, as that will affect your investment eligibility. There are several factors that affect how much you can expect to make with a rental property such as location, type of home, short-term vacation leasing or long-term living leasing, leasing to multiple tenants or one tenant for a smaller price usually, maintenance costs, unexpected vacancies, taxes, closing costs, commissions when selling etc. But depending on where you would be looking to buy, you may find that it is a lot of hassle and responsibility to become a real estate investor and there is a very high possibility that your investments will underperform investing in the Nasdaq 100, which is significantly easier to invest in. Also, for building wealth over the longterm, money can sit in the stock market growing for decades with no taxes incurring and then be sold at a lower capital gains tax rate than income tax (Fernando). Whereas, rental income is still taxable at the higher income tax rate, despite expenses you can write off. Remember, that generally, the higher someone rises from the middle class, the less of their portfolio will be made up of real estate and the more it will be stocks, and private business ownership for entrepreneurs.

STOCK MARKET

Notes

Pros:
    High potential returns (**10-12%+ annually**)
    Passive
    Low tax from lower capital gains (investment appreciation) taxation rates (Fernando). *Search current capital gains tax rate online.
Cons:
    Extremely inconsistent returns
    High volatility

These are the major stock market indexes with the S and P 500 being the most popular: S and P 500 (500 biggest U.S public companies), Nasdaq Composite (over 3,000 stocks listed on Nasdaq), Nasdaq 100 (biggest 100 companies listed on Nasdaq), DOW 30 (30 large, prominent, publicly-traded U.S. companies), Russell 2000 (2000 small cap, publicly-traded U.S. companies) (Banton, 2022). Even if you do not live in the U.S., U.S. stock indexes are still a good idea to invest in because they are where the attention primarily is globally. Total return refers to the combined returns from both the stock price appreciation and dividends (earnings distributions from the companies). If you do your own research (which is encouraged), be sure to seek out these charts online as they are harder to find than regular price charts. Total return data for the S and P 500 only goes back to about1990, and for other indexes it is even more recent, so data since January 2004 is emphasized to compare the indexes most effectively.

Average Annual Total Return of S and P 500 ("S&P 500 (^SPX)" 2023):
1990-2023: 9.7%
2004-2023: 8.88%
Note: Referring to its price chart (instead of total return chart), it didn't make new highs for 25 years from 1929 to 1954, and for 13 years from 2000 to 2013, and for 7 years 1973 to 1980 ("S&P 500 (^GSPC)," 2022).

Average Annual Total Return of Total Stock Market ("Vanguard Total Stock," 2023):
2004-2023: 8.97% (roughly tied SP500 for same period)

Average Annual Total Return of Nasdaq Composite ("Fidelity® Nasdaq Composite," 2023):
2004-2023: 10.04%

Average Annual Total Return of Nasdaq 100 ("Invesco QQQ," 2023):
2004-2023: 11.9%

Average Annual Total Return of Dow 30 ("Dow Jones Industrial Average," 2023):
2004-2023: 12.4%

Average Annual Total Return of Russell 2000 ("Russell 2000 (^Rut)," 2023):
2004-2023: 7.66%

This is not mainstream information, and it is vital. **There are multiple reasons to avoid trying to beat the market (S and P 500) by stock picking, but historically the Nasdaq Composite, Nasdaq 100, and Dow 30 have outperformed it since 2004, with the latter two performing the best and similarly to each other. It is**

very possible they will continue to outperform the S and P 500, but not guaranteed.

Reasons Not to Pick Stocks

1. Low probability of success: almost 90% of fund managers (professional stock pickers) can't beat the market in the long term and it is up to speculation if the 10% who do, do so to a degree of significance (Gunnars, 2020). Since the Nasdaq 100 does historically outperform the market, the percentage of fund managers that beat that index over a long period is likely tiny. And even if they did, after their fees for managing the fund, you most certainly would be better off investing directly in the Nasdaq 100.

2. **It is a huge misconception that stock price will correlate to company growth in the long run.** Even mid to large cap stocks can go 7+ years of diverging significantly from the revenue growth of their underlying companies. Before I learned this lesson, I lost thousands investing in stocks of companies with revenues doubling in size while their stocks would drop 90%+ over the timespan of several years!

3. It's completely normal for a stock that will grow to have a Price to Sales ratio (ratio of total stock value to revenue) between 1 and 10, so determining if one is overbought or oversold can be extremely inaccurate ("NASDAQ (NDAQ) - P/S Ratio," 2022). In other words, a company with a P/S ratio of 10 could have its stock value drop 90% and it could be arguably fairly valued afterwards, but it could also completely reasonably go up significantly and still not be considered overvalued compared to other growth stocks.

4. Historical performance of individual stocks is a very poor indicator of future performance (IWB, 2018). You can research what were the top 10 stocks by market cap, by year, and it can be observed how difficult it would have been to predict that those stocks would perform well, as well as how they consistently have gotten cycled out of the top 10 and eventually tend to stop performing notably well (IWB, 2018).

5. Taxes every time you sell a stock for a profit, unless it's in a retirement account ("Retirement Accounts Explained," 2022). If you just hold an index, its holdings can change and adapt without you paying taxes, but your individual stock portfolio (collection) is subject to taxation every time you rebalance it or replace stocks in it (Moore, et al, 2022).

6. You don't know if you're good at stock picking until at least over a decade has passed. It will be difficult to maintain emotional endurance because it's uncharted territory for you with no strong historical data to support confidence in your investments.

7. Not worth stress of risk and uncertainty for most people.

How to Pick Stocks

If you do try to pick stocks (which you shouldn't), consider:
1. Diversifying into at least 7-10 stocks or many more for a safer portfolio
2. Investing in companies you have heard of and are familiar with
3. Common sense (will the product and/or company be MORE prevalent in the future than now?)
4. History of yearly revenue growth (Over 20% ideally)
5. Reasonable P/S ratio (under 10 ideally)
6. Reasonably significant revenue numbers (at least several hundred million dollars annually, don't invest in penny stocks)
7. Past stock growth (Less important, is the stock already growing at a steady, healthy pace?)

Mutual Funds

A mutual fund is a fund in which professional managers seek to outperform the market mainly through picking stocks (Moore, et al, 2022). Index funds or Exchange Traded Funds (investment vehicles that track an underlying index and tend to be more convenient to invest in than actual index funds) tend to be a better investment for the stock market portion of a portfolio because they have more historical data that is far more likely to indicate future performance than the historical data of a mutual fund (Moore, et al, 2022). Exactly how a mutual fund is being managed can change over time as it is affected by whoever is managing it, which you have no control over. Mutual funds can have higher management fees because they are actively managed as well (Moore, et al, 2022). Also, as discussed, the vast majority of stock pickers fail to beat the market anyway. However, since mutual funds are usually diversified with many stocks, the returns of many of them may still be close to that of the overall market and other major indexes that are also diversified. This is because the more stocks are in a collection, the more the collection will perform similarly to the market, generally. With index funds or ETFs, you are investing in the long-term demand for, or the popularity of, that index and the stocks in it. With mutual funds, you are generally investing in strangers' abilities to pick stocks.

IRAs and 401Ks

Retirement accounts like IRAs and 401ks can be very advantageous for investment capital you are willing to keep invested until you are at least 60-65 years old. They are typically invested in stocks and bonds and you can control their investments, although 401Ks are usually limited to a small number of investment funds to choose from ("Retirement Accounts Explained," 2022). These accounts have different tax advantages and other benefits, but there are generally penalties for withdrawing earnings before 60, so it is important to keep them invested ("Retirement Accounts Explained," 2022).

Traditional IRA: allows you to invest up to a certain amount each year (about $6,000 today) of your pretax income (so you don't have to pay taxes on income you invest) and then at retirement you are taxed on the earnings of the account based on your income bracket at that point ("Retirement Accounts Explained," 2022).

Roth IRA: allows you to invest up to a certain amount each year (about $6,000) of your after tax income, and then all of your earnings are tax free at retirement ("Retirement Accounts Explained," 2022). If you expect to be in a higher tax bracket at retirement, then the Roth IRA will be a better choice than traditional IRA because you pay taxes early with a low tax rate vs later with a high tax rate ("Retirement Accounts Explained," 2022).

401k: is like a traditional IRA where you can invest pretax income and then pay taxes on earnings at retirement at your then-current tax rate, but it is offered to employees by certain companies ("Retirement Accounts Explained," 2022). The big benefit of a 401k over a traditional IRA however, is that the contribution limits are much higher (about $19,500 per year) and many employers offer a contribution match where they match a percentage of your contributions up to a certain limit ("Retirement Accounts Explained," 2022). This enables you to invest with extra capital, making this likely to be the best type of retirement account if your employer has a good contribution match. If you are limited in which funds you can pick from in your 401k, pick high performing funds that are most similar to the Nasdaq 100.

Leveraged ETFs

The following is not mainstream information. One very high risk strategy with limited historical data is investing in leveraged index ETFs that may either double or triple the daily performance of an underlying index (Graytok, 2022). During large market crashes these can easily lose 90% of their value or more, but they can also see massive gains during recovery ("ProShares UltraPro QQQ," 2023). They are leveraged based on the daily performance of the index, so over the long term, a double leveraged ETF may not exactly double the annual return rate of the index for example, but some of these ETFs have massively outperformed the market since they were incepted (Graytok, 2022). They have all the diversification of the underlying indexes, they are just much more volatile because they multiply daily price movements.. One investing strategy could be to allocate a percentage, such as half or one third, of whatever you are willing to invest in the stock market into a leveraged ETF depending on your risk tolerance. So if you would be comfortable investing 30% of your net worth in the Nasdaq 100, for example, instead you could invest 10% or so in the triple leveraged ETF and keep the remaining 20% in cash/CDs for when the market crashes and there is an exceptional buying opportunity. The triple leveraged Nasdaq 100 ETF is the best-performing leveraged ETF that tracks a major index as of now ("ProShares UltraPro QQQ," 2023). It is especially lucrative to capitalize on big drops because aggressive market recoveries are leveraged and compounded so having some cash on the sidelines for when the market drops 20%+ could be very beneficial. The S and P 500 has dropped 19.9% or more 11 times between 1955 and 2020 ("S&P 500 (^GSPC)," 2022, Short, 2012). The drops averaged 34.3% from highs, with the biggest drop being 56.8% ("S&P 500 (^GSPC) Historical Data.," 2022). Those bear markets (periods of price decline) averaged about 12.6 months from peak to bottom, with the longest one being 2 years and 4 months ("S&P 500 (^GSPC) Historical Data.," 2022). You could have capital ready to invest incrementally as the market reaches drops of 25%, 35%, 40%, 45%, and 50% for example, depending on if you want to risk more from investing in shorter drops or risk less from waiting for bigger drops that might not happen. You could also invest incrementally based on time instead of percentage drop, being mindful of the average bear market length. It also lowers your risk. If you invest $30k in the Nasdaq 100 and it drops 50% during a recession, you lose $15k in value, but if you invest $10k in the triple leveraged ETF and it drops 95%, you only lose $9,500 in value and have over $20k to invest and catch the leveraged recovery with. Plus, you could have been making an extra small return from keeping that cash in CDs. Based on the limited historical data we have, a one-third investment in a triple leveraged index ETF could very reasonably outperform a three-thirds investment in the non-leveraged index over the long term. For example, the Nasdaq 100 yielded almost an 8 times return between Feb 2010 and Feb 2023, but the triple leveraged version yielded almost a 57 times return. That means you could have seen the same return from investing just over 1/7th of your capital in the leveraged ETF as 100% of your capital in the non-leveraged ETF.

Average Annual Leveraged ETF Returns Since Inceptions (Total Returns):
> July 2006-January 2023
>> **SP500: 9.11%** ("S&P 500 (^SPX)" 2023)
>> **SSO (double leveraged ETF symbol): 11.24%** ("ProShares Ultra S&P500" 2023)

> November 2008-January 2023:
>> **SP500: 12.46%** ("S&P 500 (^SPX)" 2023)
>> **SPXL (triple leveraged symbol): 22.82%** (Direxion Daily S&P500® Bull 3X, 2023)

> June 2006-February 2023
>> **Nasdaq 100: 14.17%** ("Invesco QQQ," 2023)
>> **QLD (double leveraged symbol): 20.76%** ("ProShares Ultra QQQ," 2023)

> February 2010-February 2023
>> **Nasdaq 100: 17.23%** ("Invesco QQQ," 2023)
>> **TQQQ (triple leveraged symbol): 36.49%** ("ProShares UltraPro QQQ," 2023)

Strategy

Invest for the long term and avoid short term trading due to extremely low probability of success. Avoid stock picking and invest in well-known indexes/ETFs. For long-term investing, most well-known online stock brokers will work well to invest in any stock-related investment vehicle or CDs (discussed later), and also offer IRA account types. Utilize dollar cost averaging, where you invest incrementally for a period instead of investing lump sums all at once. For example, invest a set percentage of whatever you save every month. Take advantage of retirement accounts unless you have aggressive financial goals you plan to achieve before the age of 60, in which case you may not want to lock away your capital until then. Despite their dominant popularity, the S and P 500 and total stock market index simply have had relatively low average returns, compared to some other major indexes. For better, but still safe, historically proven long term stock market investing, consider investing in either the Nasdaq 100 index or the Dow 30 index, which have historically performed similarly to each other, but the Nasdaq 100 is more diversified and may contain more relevant stocks so I'd recommend it over the Dow 30. For potentially safe, higher reward, less-historically proven long-term investing, consider investing some of your stock market portfolio allowance in the triple leveraged or double leveraged Nasdaq 100 ETFs and keeping the rest in cash/short term CDs to buy market crashes. But the more of your portfolio you invest in leveraged ETFs while the market is not in a decline from its all time highs, the bigger of a drop you should wait for to invest the remaining cash you have ready for buying crashes. Do your own research and compare charts of leveraged ETFs against their underlying indexes on short, medium, and long-term time frames to determine how/if you want to incorporate them. Based on historical data, the Nasdaq 100 index and Dow 30 index can be comparable in returns, and the S and P 500 underperforms them.

CERTIFICATES OF DEPOSIT AND ANNUITIES

Notes

Pros:
 Extremely safe
 Guaranteed, consistent income
Cons:
 Tie up your money for months to years
 Low returns

Strategy

Consider keeping most of your cash that you don't plan on using for at least a couple months in CDs or high interest savings accounts or brokerage accounts that reflect similar rates to CDs without the time commitment.. They are certificates issued by a bank to a person depositing money for a specified length of time (Fernando, et al, 2022). You have to keep your money invested in them for the specified length of time or you may pay a penalty for early withdrawal (Fernando, et al, 2022). Return rates offered by CDs can fluctuate depending on factors such as the federal funds rate and are likely to offer better returns when the federal funds rate is higher (Fernando, et al, 2022). Regardless, historically, they have outperformed savings and money market accounts and the top CDs can outperform bonds as well without any of the volatility that bonds have (Fernando, et al, 2022). Top CDs currently pay out about 3-4% annually for 3 month to 1 year terms and 4-4.5% for 1-5 year terms (Karl, et al, 2022). They are a great way to help protect the buying power of your cash from inflation.

Another somewhat similar type of investment is an annuity. There are many different versions of annuities with various terms depending on what company you get them through and which one you pick. However, the general idea is that you give a lump sum of money to an insurance company that offers annuities and they provide you with guaranteed income that may be for the rest of your life or for a fixed number of years, depending on the terms (Hicks, 2023). Some can even pay out to your heirs after you die (Hicks, 2023). A realistic annual return can be around 5% (Hicks, 2023). This makes them a potentially ideal investment for retirement when CD rates are lower and you are looking for a guaranteed stream of income with a guaranteed interest rate. However, the major drawback is putting up the lump sum and not being able to withdraw it because it will only be repaid as regular payments over the course of time.

NICHOLAS SOVIA

CRYPTOCURRENCY, ART, PRECIOUS METALS, COMMODITIES

These investment vehicles tend to be very unreliable, unpredictable, volatile, and inconsistent and most arguably have very little fundamental value, in general ("Bitcoin USD (BTC-USD)," 2022, "Silver Mar 23 (Si=F)," 2022). Businesses and real estate, for example, offer desired and needed products and services, therefore they have fundamental value. Stocks can be thought of as a degree removed from their underlying companies and don't always directly correlate with the value fluctuations of their underlying businesses, so they tend to be based on less fundamental value than private businesses, but they still represent ownership of real businesses that provide value at the end of the day. The values of cryptocurrencies, art, precious metals, and commodities, however, are determined mostly by unpredictable collective consciousness and perception instead of fundamental value and needs, therefore they are arguably much worse investment vehicles and typically fall into a small speculative portion of a portfolio. But it could be argued that if a speculative portion of a portfolio isn't significant enough to make or break your portfolio, then perhaps there's no point in having that portion in it at all. And these particular investment vehicles may be more likely to break your portfolio than make it. Some cryptocurrencies, such as

Ethereum, have technological applicability beyond just being used as virtual currencies, and these are more promising than other cryptocurrencies due to their potential fundamental value (Frankenfield, 2022). But they are still very risky investments and their fad-based and very limited history makes them even riskier.

HOW TO ACHIEVE
FINANCIAL SUCCESS

APPROACHES

1. *No Career Chosen:* If you have no idea what to do for a career or what to do with your capital, keep most of it in CDs and experiment with, and research and reflect on different career paths until you gain some direction for your career. Consider investing a small amount of it in leveraged index ETFs if you can handle losing it, but keep most of it in cash/CDs so you have capital to pursue whatever career you end up choosing. Avoid unrealistic, get-rich-quick approaches and use common sense. Work a basic job in the meantime.

2. *Career Chosen, Not Attained:* If you think you know what career(s) you would like to pursue, but haven't pursued them yet, invest most of your capital in obtaining the necessary education/certifications etc. to make it or them a reality. Work a basic job in the meantime.

3. *Chosen Career Attained to Some Extent:* If you are already working your chosen career, the question you must ask yourself is whether or not your career is scalable. If it is, like a business, in the sense that you can invest money into it and see growth and return, then that should probably be your main investment unless the potential returns are expected to be smaller than alternative investments. If it is not scalable, and it is a job with fixed pay for example, then you will want to invest as much as you can, within reason, in the Nasdaq 100 (either leveraged or regular depending on your risk tolerance) and optional real estate. If your income is not likely to grow substantially anytime soon and you are comfortable living in one city for multiple years, then the first time

home buyer loan which allows you to buy a home with as little as a 3.5% down payment may be a good investment you can make if you are eligible, especially if you can have roommates to pay you rent ("First-Time Home Buyer Programs," 2022). If your income may grow significantly in the near future, then you may not want to invest in a less expensive home now, and instead wait until you can afford a nicer one (if real estate is something you are interested in).

NOTES AND EXAMPLE

Please note that settling for an income you can't save at least several thousand dollars per year, and that is unlikely to grow significantly, will make it potentially very challenging for you to ever achieve significant financial success, depending on your goals, age, and current savings. The lower your income is, the more frugally you will have to live to achieve success without career changes. Depending on your financial goals, ideal time for achieving them, and how much you are earning in your work, you may have to take on more or less risk and volatility to achieve them. You can use a compound interest calculator to estimate how much you will have to invest, your necessary returns, and number of years for success, and be sure to account for inflation. Financial success is relative, and finding a valuable career you mostly enjoy that earns good income and utilizes your talents is probably the best and most attainable financial goal. It is possible to build wealth without adding value, but that approach usually fails and is just a temptation to mostly avoid. Simply setting the intention to make most of your money from adding value will automatically protect you from having to learn an array of tough financial lessons the hard way. The perfect balance between adding value and exercising financial intelligence to take care of yourself is where the money is likely best made. But note that as far as retirement goes, about $2.5 million without social security or pensions is the number where you can realistically make around $100k per year in a retirement portfolio diversified between optional real estate, CDs , and annuities, as well as index funds/ETFs. **One can expect to earn about 4% per year (after 3% inflation protection) of whatever their net worth is in passive income,** maybe a little more if rental properties are utilized instead of REITs.

Example:

This example is based on the minimum savings and invest-ment requirements for a 30 year old planning to retire at age 65 via $60k in inflation-adjusted passive income who makes $60k per year at their job and an expected (potentially pessimistic) 8.5% average annual return on their stock and real estate invest-ments, who maximally utilizes their (Roth) IRA/401k, and who invests 80% of their savings, keeping the other 20% in cash/CDs. If you start making say about $24k a year from social security at age 65, then you will only need $36k from passive investments to make $60k a year passively (adjusted for inflation). Therefore, with a retirement portfolio like the one shown later, you will need a net worth of about $1m after you pay taxes on converting your growth portfolio into a retirement income portfolio.

Net worth goal: about $1.1m before taxes, $1m after taxes (ad-justed for 3% inflation, assuming 10% taxes rebalancing portfolio from growth-focused to retirement-focused).

By age: 65

Current age: 30

Current investable savings: $0

Realistic necessary income: at least $60k

Necessary average yearly savings: $15,500 for first 17.5 years, $26,000 for remaining 17.5 years due to income growth from inflation

Average annual return: 8.5% (this could definitely be higher if you invest in indexes that outperform the S and P 500 or in good real estate investments)

This is a mostly safe, realistic approach to retire at 65 with a $60k annual income if you are still 30 or younger and can afford to save and invest about 26% of your income. Unfortunately for many, this is more than they make, or they may be older than 30, or they may have children and various unavoidable expenses that prevent them from being able to save 26% of that income. Also, perhaps you would like to enjoy a greater level of retirement income, like $100k per year instead of $60k, which would require annual savings of more like $30,000 instead of $15,500, which may require an income of more like $80k+. Therefore, the feasible way to achieve significantly more aggressive financial goals without career changes is to risk the incorporation of leveraged ETFs into your portfolio.

PORTFOLIO IDEAS FOR ALLOCATING NET WORTH AND SAVED INCOME

Many factors will affect what portfolio and approach is right for you, such as:

1. Age
2. Risk tolerance
3. Level of desire and urgency for greater wealth
4. Where market is in relation to all time highs, as well as the last bear market
5. Whether you are entrepreneurially-focused or day job-focused

For example, if you are older, love your job, and the market is at all time highs and hasn't had a bear market in ten years, you probably don't want to be investing half your net worth in leveraged ETFs. But if the market is down 30%+ from highs and you are young and eager to cultivate mass wealth without a business, that could be a great time to take on some risk with heavily investing in TQQQ and then consider transitioning from TQQQ to QLD later as the market hits all time highs again. TQQQ's returns are historically unparalleled, but if a crash like 2008 happens again, it will probably be completely wiped out (most likely a percentage drop in the high 90s). QLD, however, was around in 2008 and we know its drop was around 85%, which is far more recoverable as a close-to-worst case scenario ("ProShares Ultra QQQ," 2023). As a result,

QLD is a better buy and hold option over long periods. But TQQQ is excellent for buying bear markets with money you are willing to risk entirely. With all of this in mind, you need to strongly reflect on what you want to do based on these factors, while referencing a compound interest calculator and historical ETF data. The ideal approach is highly personalized so this book can't tell you exactly what to do. But generally, perhaps consider a focus on TQQQ and QLD during bear markets and a focus on cash and QLD during all time highs. And, if possible and applicable, getting your full 401k match in addition to these riskier approaches is really ideal to have something to fall back on in your 60s if all else fails. Also, if you want to see significant wealth growth, portfolio percentages will need to be flexible. You will need to think more in terms of trades with profit targets at which you rebalance your portfolio, instead of keeping your portfolio as set allocation percentages like in the examples below. So for example, you might buy the dip of a bear market with some TQQQ and QLD with $100k of your $150k net worth (pretty aggressive move), and then you rebalance your portfolio once you hit $500k. There's a growth period of "letting it ride" where your portfolio percentages get heavily skewed toward the growth drivers (leveraged ETFs). The $50k you had outside the market was 33% of your net worth at the start, but right before the rebalance, it was only 10%. However, the game is different in retirement where you may find yourself regularly rebalancing your portfolio to keep it in line with target allocation percentages. This is because you want that consistent income and you are not trying to push wealth brackets. Rebalancing a portfolio every year without ever letting it ride is likely to butcher compounded gains for a growth-focused portfolio. Those "let it ride" stages can be what define your wealth bracket more than just about anything. It's all a matter of what you want to do, and there's absolutely nothing wrong with taking the 30+ year road to retirement at a career you like, investing in non-leveraged Nasdaq, S and P, and lower-risk 401k funds, and perhaps getting a mortgage and whatnot. There is something to be said for not having your 20s, 30s etc. be dominated by sleepless nights from all the risk you are taking.

Portfolio #1-Entrepreneurial High Growth
    50-60% business
    0-20% Triple and/or double leveraged Nasdaq 100 index
    25-45% CDs
    5% cash
A lot of cash ready to invest in business, and ETF during crashes

Portfolio #2-Entrepreneurial Diversified 1:
    40% business
    0-20% real estate
    20-40% Nasdaq 100 index and/or Dow 30 index
    15% CDs
    5% cash

Portfolio #3-Entrepreneurial Diversified 2:
    40% business
    0-20% real estate
    10-30% Triple and/or double leveraged Nasdaq 100 index
    25% CDs (Invest 10% in ETF during market crashes)
    5% cash

Portfolio #4-Entrepreneurial Retirement:
    0-40% Triple leveraged, double leveraged, or non-leveraged Nasdaq 100 index
    10-60% business
    20-40% real estate
    20-45% CDs/annuities
    5% cash

Note* depending on what stage you are at in your business, you may want to strictly focus your funds between your business and having cash available for your business, as other investments may spread you too thin to be successful as an entrepreneur.

Portfolio #5-Worker's High Growth:
    40-60% Triple and/or double leveraged Nasdaq 100 index
    45-55% CDs (Invest 30-40% in ETF during market crashes)

5% cash

Portfolio #6-Worker's Safe Longterm 1:

    0-50% real estate

    30-80% Nasdaq 100 index and/or Dow 30 index

    15% CDs

    5% cash

Portfolio #7-Worker's Safe Longterm 2:

    40-50% real estate

    10-20% Triple and/or double leveraged Nasdaq 100 index

    25-35% CDs (Invest up to 20% during market crashes)

    5% cash

Portfolio #8-Worker's Retirement:

    0-30% Triple and/or double leveraged Nasdaq 100 index

    20-60% real estate

    35-45% CDs/annuities

    5% cash

Portfolio #9-Worker's Retirement 2:

    60% Nasdaq 100

    10% real estate

    25% CDs/annuities

    5% cash

Note* for a retirement portfolio like #9, it is important to live off of a small percentage (4% for example) because you do not want to have to sell your stock during a market crash because you need it to live. You want enough stable and liquid cash/CDs to live several years during market downturns and then always sell stock near all time highs. Also, for high-growth non-entrepreneurial portfolios, another option is, instead of having a set percentage of the portfolio in cash, you can have a set amount of cash and just invest everything above that. But then you may have a smaller fund for emergencies and capitalizing on drops and investment opportunities.

REVIEW REMINDER

Thank you for reading. Your time taken to read this guide is greatly appreciated and your opinion is valued. Please consider leaving a review on Amazon to help the creator and potential future readers.

BIBLIOGRAPHY

1. "Finding a Business Broker." Transworld Business Advisors, https://www.tworld.com/sell-a-business/seller-faq/how-much-can-I-sell-my-business-for/#:~:text=A%20business%20will%20likely%20sell%20for%20two%20to,will%20sell%20for%20is%20determining%20its%20market%20value.

2. Gustafson, Katherine. "The Percentage of Businesses That Fail." LendingTree, 2 May 2022, https://www.lendingtree.com/business/small/failure-rate/.

3. The Motley Fool. "How to Invest in Venture Capital." Nasdaq, 5 June 2017, https://www.nasdaq.com/articles/how-invest-venture-capital-2017-06-05.

4. Goodshore, Chloe. "Angel Investors vs. Venture Capitalists." Business.org, 25 July 2022, https://www.business.org/finance/loans/what-is-the-difference-between-an-angel-investor-and-venture-capitalist/.

5. "Dividing the Pie: How Venture Fund Economics Work [Part II]." Seraf, https://seraf-investor.com/compass/article/dividing-pie-how-venture-fund-economics-work-part-ii.

6. PK. "Historical US Home Prices: Monthly Median from 1953-2022." DQYDJ, 16 Oct. 2022, https://dqydj.com/historical-home-prices/.

7. Nicely, Tyler. "How Much Rent to Charge for Your Property: Zillow Rental Manager." Rentals Resource Center, Zillow, 10 Feb.2021,https://www.zillow.com/rental-manager/resources/how-much-can-i-rent-my-house-for/#5.

8. "First-Time Home Buyer Programs: Explore 2023 Grants and Loans: Zillow." Home Buyers Guide, 7 Dec. 2022, https://www.zillow.com/home-buying-guide/first-time-buyer-loan-programs/#h_2_6.

9. Mortgage.info. "Minimum Home Equity Needed for a Mortgage Refinance." Mortgage.info, 18 Feb. 2022, https://mortgage.info/much-home-equity-need-refinance-mortgage/.

10. Chen, James. "Real Estate Investment Trust (REIT): How They Work and How to Invest." Investopedia, Investopedia, 19 Dec. 2022, https://www.investopedia.com/terms/r/reit.asp.

11. Vandenboss, Kevin. "4 Non-Traded REITs to Consider Adding to Your Portfolio." Yahoo! Finance, Yahoo!, 23 Sept. 2021, https://finance.yahoo.com/news/4-non-traded-reits-consider-151331482.html?fr=yhssrp_catchall&guccounter=1.

12. Morris, Chad. "Fundrise.com Review (2023)." Brokerage Reviews,https://www.brokerage-review.com/article/account/fundrise-review.aspx#:~:text=Fundrise%20Returns%20Fundrise%20historically%20has%20seen%20annualized%20returns,the%20form%20of%20asset%20appreciation%20or%20dividend%20distributions.
13. Boone, Ali. "20 Can't-Miss Rental Property Write Offs." | BiggerPockets Blog, 4 Mar. 2017, https://www.biggerpockets.com/blog/rental-tax-write-offs.

14. Fernando, Jason. "Capital Gains Tax: What It Is, How It Works, and Current Rates." Investopedia. Investopedia, 30 July 2022. Web. 13 Oct. 2022, https://www.investopedia.com/terms/c/cap-

ital_gains_tax.asp.

15. Banton, Caroline. "An Introduction to U.S. Stock Market Indexes." Investopedia. Investopedia, 29 Mar. 2022. Web. 13 Oct. 2022,https://www.investopedia.com/insights/introduction-to-stock-market-indices/.

16. "S&P 500 (^GSPC) Historical Data." Yahoo! Finance, Yahoo!, 30 Dec. 2022, https://finance.yahoo.com/quote/%5EGSPC/history?period1=-1325635200&period2=1672358400&interval=1mo&filter=history&frequency=1mo&includeAdjustedClose=true.

17. "S&P 500 (^SPX)." Y Charts, 10 Feb. 2023, https://ycharts.com/indices/%5ESPX/chart/#/?annualizedReturns=true&calcs=id:total_return_forward_adjusted_price,include:true,,&chartId=&chartType=interactive&correlations=&customGrowthAmount=&dateSelection=range&displayDateRange=false&endDate=&format=real&legendOnChart=false&lineAnnotations=&nameInLegend=name_and_ticker&note=&partner=basic_2000&quoteLegend=false&recessions=false&scaleType=linear&securities=id:%5ESPX,include:true,,&securityGroup=&securitylistName=&securitylistSecurityId=&source=false&splitType=single&startDate=&title=&units=false&useCustomColors=false&useEstimates=false&zoom=max&redesign=true&chartAnnotations=&axisExtremes=

18. "Vanguard Total Stock Market ETF (VTI)." Y Charts, 10 Feb. 2023, https://ycharts.com/companies/VTI/chart/#/?annualizedReturns=true&calcs=id:total_return_forward_adjusted_price,include:true,,&chartId=&chartType=interactive&correlations=&customGrowthAmount=&dateSelection=range&displayDateRange=false&endDate=01%2F01%2F2023&format=real&legendOnChart=false&lineAnnotations=&nameInLegend=name_and_ticker&note=&partner=basic_2000&quoteLegend=false&recessions=false&scaleType=linear&securities=id:VTI,include:true,,&se

curityGroup=&securitylistName=&securitylistSecurityId=&sour
ce=false&splitType=single&startDate=01%2F01%2F2004&title=
&units=false&useCustomColors=false&useEstimates=false&zoo
m=custom&redesign=true&chartAnnotations=&axisExtremes=

19. "Fidelity® Nasdaq Composite ETF (ONEQ)." Y Charts, 10 Feb.
2023, https://ycharts.com/companies/ONEQ/chart/#/?
annualizedReturns=true&calcs=id:total_return_forward_adjuste
d_price,include:true,,&chartId=&chartType=interactive&correlat
ions=&customGrowthAmount=&dateSelection=range&displayD
ateRange=false&endDate=01%2F01%2F2023&format=real&lege
ndOnChart=false&lineAnnotations=&nameInLegend=name_and
_ticker&note=&partner=basic_2000&quoteLegend=false&recessi
ons=false&scaleType=linear&securities=id:ONEQ,include:true,,
&securityGroup=&securitylistName=&securitylistSecurityId=&s
ource=false&splitType=single&startDate=01%2F01%2F2004&ti
tle=&units=false&useCustomColors=false&useEstimates=false&
zoom=custom&redesign=true&chartAnnotations=&axisExtrem
es=

20. "Invesco QQQ Trust (QQQ)." Y Charts, 10 Feb. 2023, https://
ycharts.com/companies/QQQ/chart/#/?
annualizedReturns=true&calcs=id:total_return_forward_adjuste
d_price,include:true,,&chartId=&chartType=interactive&correlat
ions=&customGrowthAmount=&dateSelection=range&displayD
ateRange=false&endDate=01%2F01%2F2023&format=real&lege
ndOnChart=false&lineAnnotations=&nameInLegend=name_and
_ticker&note=&partner=basic_2000&quoteLegend=false&recessi
ons=false&scaleType=linear&securities=id:QQQ,include:true,,&s
ecurityGroup=&securitylistName=&securitylistSecurityId=&sou
rce=false&splitType=single&startDate=01%2F01%2F2004&title
=&units=false&useCustomColors=false&useEstimates=false&zo
om=custom&redesign=true&chartAnnotations=&axisExtremes
=

21. "Dow Jones Industrial Average (^DJI)." Y Charts, 10 Feb. 2023,

https://ycharts.com/indices/%5EDJI/chart/#/?
annualizedReturns=true&calcs=id:total_return_forward_adjuste
d_price,include:true,,&chartId=&chartType=interactive&correlat
ions=&customGrowthAmount=&dateSelection=range&displayD
ateRange=false&endDate=01%2F01%2F2023&format=real&lege
ndOnChart=false&lineAnnotations=&nameInLegend=
name_and_ticker&note=&partner=basic_2000&quoteLegend=fal
se&recessions=false&scaleType=linear&securities=id:
%5EDJI,include:true,,&securityGroup=&securitylistName=&secu
ritylistSecurityId=&source=false&splitType=single&startDate=
01%2F01%2F2004&title=&units=false&useCustomColors=false
&useEstimates=false&zoom=custom&redesign=true&chartAn-
notations=&axisExtremes=

22. "Russell 2000 (^RUT)." Y Charts, 10 Feb. 2023, https://ychart-
s.com/indices/%5ERUT/chart/#/?
annualizedReturns=true&calcs=id:total_return_forward_adjuste
d_price,include:true,,&chartId=&chartType=interactive&correlat
ions=&customGrowthAmount=&dateSelection=range&displayD
ateRange=false&endDate=01%2F01%2F2023&format=real&lege
ndOnChart=false&lineAnnotations=&nameInLegend=
name_and_ticker&note=&partner=basic_2000&quoteLegend=fal
se&recessions=false&scaleType=linear&securities=id:
%5ERUT,include:true,,&securityGroup=&securitylistName=&sec
uritylistSecurityId=&source=false&splitType=single&startDate=
01%2F01%2F2004&title=&units=false&useCustomColors=false
&useEstimates=false&zoom=custom&redesign=true&chartAn-
notations=&axisExtremes=

23. Gunnars, Kris. "Is It True That Almost No One Can Beat the
Market?" Stock Analysis, 8 May 2020, https://stockanalysis.com/
article/can-you-beat-the-market/.

24. "NASDAQ (NDAQ) - P/S Ratio." CompaniesMarketCap.com -
Companies Ranked by Market Capitalization, 2022, https://
companiesmarketcap.com/nasdaq/ps-ratio/

#:~:text=P%2FS%20ratio%20for%20Nasdaq%20%28NDAQ%29 %20P%2FS%20ratio%20as,the%20company%27s%20cur- rent%20price-to-sales%20ratio%20%28TT- M%29%20is%204.75922.

25. Iwb. "Largest Companies in the World by Market Cap, 1980 to Today." Investment Watch, 16 Sept. 2018, https://www.invest- mentwatchblog.com/largest-companies-in-the-world-by-mar- ket-cap-1980-to-today/

26. -Moore, Barry D, et al. "ETFs vs. Mutual Funds vs. Index Funds: Simply Explained." Liberated Stock Trader, 4 Jan. 2022, https:// www.liberatedstocktrader.com/etf-vs-mutual-funds-vs-index- fund/
#:~:text=If%20an%20ETF%20tracks%20an%20index%2C%20it %20is,be%20either%20an%20ETF%20or%20a%20mu- tual%20fund.

27. "Retirement Accounts Explained." Liberty Group, LLC, 7 Jan. 2022, https://libertygroupllc.com/retirement-accounts-ex- plained/.

28. Graytok, Sean. "What Is TQQQ? Overview & How to Use It." SimpleMoneyLyfe, 23 July 2022, https://simplemoneylyfe.com/ investing/what-is-tqqq/
#:~:text=The%20ProShares%20UltraPro%20QQQ%2C%20more %20commonly%20referred%20to,the%20popular- ity%20of%20the%20underlying%20index%20it%20follows.

29. "ProShares Ultra S&P500 (SSO)."Y Charts, 10 Feb. 2023, https://ycharts.com/companies/SSO/chart/#/? annualizedReturns=true&calcs=id:total_return_forward_adjuste d_price,include:true,,&chartId=&chartType=interactive&correlat ions=&customGrowthAmount=&dateSelection=range&displayD ateRange=false&endDate=&format=real&legendOnChart=false& lineAnnotations=&nameInLegend=name_and_ticker&note=&pa

rtner=basic_2000&quoteLegend=false&recessions=false&scaleT ype=linear&securities=id:SSO,include:true,,&securityGroup=&se curitylistName=&securitylistSecurityId=&source=fal- se&splitType=single&startDate=&title=&units=false&useCusto mColors=false&useEstimates=false&zoom=max&redesign=true &chartAnnotations=&axisExtremes=

30. "Direxion Daily S&P500® Bull 3X ETF (SPXL)." Y Charts, 10 Feb. 2023, https://ycharts.com/companies/SPXL/chart/#/? annualizedReturns=true&calcs=id:total_return_forward_adjuste d_price,include:true,,&chartId=&chartType=interactive&correlat ions=&customGrowthAmount=&dateSelection=range&displayD ateRange=false&endDate=&format=real&legendOnChart=false& lineAnnotations=&nameInLegend=name_and_ticker&note=&pa rtner=basic_2000&quoteLegend=false&recessions=false&scaleT ype=linear&securities=id:SPXL,include:true,,&securityGroup=&s ecuritylistName=&securitylistSecurityId=&source=fal- se&splitType=single&startDate=&title=&units=false&useCusto mColors=false&useEstimates=false&zoom=max&redesign=true &chartAnnotations=&axisExtremes=

31. "ProShares Ultra QQQ (QLD)." Y Charts, 10 Feb. 2023, https:// ycharts.com/companies/QLD/chart/#/? annualizedReturns=true&calcs=id:total_return_forward_adjuste d_price,include:true,,&chartId=&chartType=interactive&correlat ions=&customGrowthAmount=&dateSelection=range&displayD ateRange=false&endDate=02%2F01%2F2023&format=real&lege ndOnChart=false&lineAnnotations=&nameInLegend=name_and _ticker&note=&partner=basic_2000&quoteLegend=false&recessi ons=false&scaleType=linear&securities=id:QLD,include:true,,&s ecurityGroup=&securitylistName=&securitylistSecurityId=&sou rce=false&splitType=single&startDate=06%2F19%2F2006&title =&units=false&useCustomColors=false&useEstimates=false&zo om=custom&redesign=true&chartAnnotations=&axisExtremes =

32. "ProShares UltraPro QQQ (TQQQ)." Y Charts, 10 Feb. 2023, https://ycharts.com/companies/TQQQ/chart/#/?annualizedReturns=true&calcs=id:total_return_forward_adjuste d_price,include:true,,&chartId=&chartType=interactive&correlat ions=&customGrowthAmount=&dateSelection=range&displayD ateRange=false&endDate=&format=real&legendOnChart=false& lineAnnotations=&nameInLegend=name_and_ticker&note=&pa rtner=basic_2000&quoteLegend=false&recessions=false&scaleT ype=linear&securities=id:TQQQ,include:true,,&securityGroup=& securitylistName=&securitylistSecurityId=&source=fal- se&splitType=single&startDate=&title=&units=false&useCusto mColors=false&useEstimates=false&zoom=max&redesign=true &chartAnnotations=&axisExtremes=

33. Short, Doug. "The S&P 500 and Recessions." Financial Sense, 8 Aug. 2012, https://www.financialsense.com/contributors/doug- short/the-s-and-p-500-and-recessions.

34. Fernando, Jason, and Somer Anderson. "What Is a Certificate of Deposit (CD) and What Can It Do for You?" Investopedia, In- vestopedia, 12 Dec. 2022, https://www.investopedia.com/terms/ c/certificateofdeposit.asp.

35. Karl, Sabrina, and Michael Boyle. "The Top CD Rates for Jan- uary 2023." Investopedia, Investopedia, 30 Dec. 2022, https:// www.investopedia.com/best-cd-rates-4770214.

36. Hicks, Coryanne. "17 Things You Need to Know about Annu- ities | Investing | U.S. News." Edited by Daniel J Lee, U.S News, 14 June 2023, money.usnews.com/ investing/investing-101/articles/things-you-need-to-know-now- about-annuities.

37. "Bitcoin USD (BTC-USD) Price History & Historical Data." Yahoo! Finance, Yahoo!, 30 Dec. 2022, https://finance.yahoo.com/ quote/BTC-USD/history?

period1=1410825600&period2=1666656000&interval=1mo&fil
ter=history&frequency=1mo&includeAdjustedClose=true.

38. "Silver Mar 23 (Si=F) Stock Historical Prices & Data." Yahoo! Finance, Yahoo!, 30 Dec. 2022, https://finance.yahoo.com/quote/
SI%3DF/history?
period1=967507200&period2=1666656000&interval=1mo&filt
er=history&frequency=1mo&includeAdjustedClose=true.

39. Frankenfield, Jake. "What is Ethereum and How Does it
Work?." Investopedia, Investopedia, 27 Sept. 2022, https://www.
investopedia.com/terms/e/ethereum.asp.